The History of the Bible: The Making of the New Testament Canon

Bart D. Ehrman, Ph.D.

PUBLISHED BY:

THE GREAT COURSES
Corporate Headquarters
4840 Westfields Boulevard, Suite 500
Chantilly, Virginia 20151-2299
Phone: 1-800-832-2412
Fax: 703-378-3819
www.thegreatcourses.com

Printed in the United States of America

Bart D. Ehrman, Ph.D.

Professor of Religious Studies
The University of North Carolina at Chapel Hill

Professor Bart D. Ehrman is the James A. Gray Professor and Chair of the Department of Religious Studies at The University of North Carolina at Chapel Hill. With degrees from Wheaton College (B.A.) and Princeton Theological Seminary (M.Div. and Ph.D., magna cum laude), he taught at Rutgers for four years before moving to UNC in 1988. During his tenure at UNC, he has garnered numerous awards and prizes, including the Students' Undergraduate Teaching Award (1993), the Ruth and Philip Hettleman Prize for Artistic and Scholarly Achievement (1994), the Bowman and Gordon Gray Award for Excellence in Teaching (1998), and the James A. Gray Chair in Biblical Studies (2003).

With a focus on early Christianity in its Greco-Roman environment and a special expertise in the textual criticism of the New Testament, Professor Ehrman has published dozens of book reviews and more than 20 scholarly articles for academic journals. He has authored or edited 16 books, including *Misquoting Jesus: The Story Behind Who Changed the Bible and Why* (San Francisco: HarperSanFrancisco, 2005); *Truth and Fiction in the Da Vinci Code* (New York: Oxford University Press, 2004); *Lost Christianities: The Battles for Scripture and the Faiths We Never Knew* (New York: Oxford University Press, 2003); *Jesus: Apocalyptic Prophet of the New Millennium* (Oxford University Press, 1999); *The New Testament: A Historical Introduction to the Early Christian Writings* (Oxford, 1997; 3rd ed., 2004); and *The Orthodox Corruption of Scripture* (Oxford, 1993). He is currently at work on a new commentary on several non-canonical Gospels for the *Hermeneia Commentary* series, published by Fortress Press.

Professor Ehrman is a popular lecturer, giving numerous talks each year for such groups as the Carolina Speakers Bureau, the UNC Program for the Humanities, the Biblical Archaeology Society, and select universities across the nation. He has served as the president of the Society of Biblical Literature, Southeast Region; book review editor of the *Journal of Biblical Literature*; editor of the Scholar's Press Monograph Series *The New Testament in the Greek Fathers*; and co-editor of the E. J. Brill series *New Testament Tools and Studies*. Among his administrative responsibilities, he has served on the executive committee of the Southeast Council for the Study of Religion and has chaired the New Testament textual criticism section of the Society of Biblical Religion, as well as serving as Director of Graduate Studies and Chair of the Department of Religious Studies at UNC.

Table of Contents

The History of the Bible: The Making of the New Testament Canon

The History of the Bible: The Making of the New Testament Canon

Scope:

There can be no question that the New Testament is the most important book—or collection of books—in the history of Western civilization; it is by far the "bestseller" of all time, since the invention of printing. But many people today do not know a lot about the New Testament, including such basic facts as what books it contains, when they were written, by whom, when, and for what purpose; how the books were copied and transmitted down through the ages; and when and why they came to be collected together into a canon of Scripture.

This course is designed to answer these basic questions about the New Testament. We will begin with an overview of what the New Testament contains in broad terms. We will then move to a consideration of the earliest writings of the New Testament, the letters of the apostle Paul. En route, we will consider some basic information about how books were actually written in the ancient world, before there were word processors, photocopy machines, typewriters, or movable type. What writing materials were used? How were books published? How did they get circulated?

We will then consider Paul's letters themselves, asking why they were written, what crucial issues they address, and what message they convey. In a subsequent lecture, we will consider the circumstance that there were other letters in circulation in early Christianity that *claimed* to be written by Paul but probably weren't. This will lead us to consider the widespread phenomenon of *pseudepigraphy* (forgeries in the name of a famous person), both in the ancient world at large and in the early Christian movement itself.

From there, we will move to a consideration of the Gospels. These books differ from the Epistles in that they are not merely compositions of a single author but embody traditions about Jesus that had been in circulation by word of mouth for decades before the authors produced their accounts. We will begin our examination by asking how the oral circulation of these traditions affected them—were some of the stories in the Gospels modified from how they originally happened? Were some of them actually made up?

We will then look at the earliest Gospels we have—which are those of the New Testament, Matthew, Mark, Luke, and John—to see who their actual authors were and to understand the messages they tried to convey in their narrations of the birth, life, death, and resurrection of Jesus. As we will see, these four were not the only gospel records that we have; in our next lecture, we will examine some of the other Gospels, those that did not make it into the New Testament.

From there, we will move to a broader consideration of how these various books—Epistles, Gospels, and other writings—have come down to us today. We will look at how books were published and distributed in the ancient world and consider, in particular, how they were copied in an age in which the only way to make a new copy of a book was to reproduce it by hand, one word at a time. How did the copying processes affect the words of the text? Were the words ever changed, so that we don't know what the author originally wrote?

We will continue our investigation by asking why these various books were so widely circulated, noticing on the way that Christianity was unusual in the ancient world for placing such a heavy emphasis on literary texts as authorities for faith and practice. One problem, however, is that different Christian communities had different understandings of the faith—and all of them had "authoritative" books (allegedly by apostles) that promoted their own understandings of the faith.

The wide range of surviving "apostolic" literature is one of the factors that drove Christians to decide on a specific *canon* of Scripture, that is, one collection of books that could be accepted as providing the authoritative basis for the faith. But even agreeing on which books to include did not solve all the problems, because different readers can interpret the same text in different ways. Thus, Christians also devised rules for interpreting these sacred books.

We will conclude the course by looking at the question of when the canon came to be finalized, establishing for all time the contours of the Christian Scriptures, the New Testament as it has come down to us today.

Lecture One

The New Testament—An Overview

Scope: This course will deal with some of the most fundamental questions about the New Testament Scriptures: How did we get the 27 books of the New Testament? When and how were the books written? For what purpose? How were they circulated and transmitted? When were they collected into a canon of Scripture?

We begin, in this opening lecture, by dealing with some of the basic facts about the New Testament: which books it contains, when they were written, in what language, and by whom. This will be a good "refresher" for those who are already familiar with the Christian Scriptures and vital information for those coming to these books for the first time.

Outline

I. Despite its vast importance and popularity, the New Testament remains an "unknown book" to many highly educated people today.

   A. It is rarely read, let alone studied, outside of church settings (contrast other bestselling books!).

   B. As a result, it is accepted as authoritative much more widely than it is known.

   C. I realize this anew every year in my introductory New Testament course that I teach at UNC, when I begin the class with a pop quiz on basic information about the New Testament—with students who say they believe in the Bible but clearly don't know what is in it.

II. There can be little doubt that the New Testament is the most important book in the history of Western civilization.

   A. It lies at the foundation of the largest and culturally most significant religion in the West.

   B. It is the "book of faith" for millions of Christians still today.

C. It continues to be not only the all-time bestseller but also an important cultural artifact in popular culture, as can be seen in such movies as *The Passion of Christ* and such novels as *The Da Vinci Code*.

III. This set of lectures is meant to provide an introduction to the New Testament for people who recognize its historical and cultural importance but who have not yet had a chance to get to know where it came from, what it contains, and how it was transmitted down to us today.

A. Our focus will be on *historical* information about the New Testament; the course does not presuppose either faith or skepticism.

B. The course is designed for anyone interested in knowing more about the most important book in the history of our culture.

C. It will address some of the key questions people have about the New Testament.

1. What kinds of books does it contain?
2. When, how, and why were these books written?
3. What do these different books teach?
4. How did these books get collected into a *canon* of Scripture?
5. How did they get transmitted down through the ages until today?

IV. We can start in this lecture with some of the most basic information about the New Testament.

A. The New Testament contains 27 separate books, written by 14 or 15 early Christian authors for other Christian communities and individuals.

B. The books are our earliest surviving Christian writings of any kind, written in the 1st century A.D.

C. All the books were originally written in Greek.

1. Greek was the *lingua franca* of the early Roman Empire.
2. It was not the language of Jesus or his earliest followers (who all spoke Aramaic) but was the language of most of the Christians of the second generation, when these books started to appear.

- **D.** The books of the New Testament are arranged in four groups, according to genre.
  1. The New Testament begins with the Gospels: four accounts of the life, ministry, death, and resurrection of Jesus.
  2. It continues with the book of Acts, a historical account of the life of the Christian Church and its missionary efforts after Jesus' resurrection.
  3. It then contains 21 Epistles, actual letters written by Christian leaders, most prominently the apostle Paul, to Christian communities and individuals, dealing with problems of faith and living.
  4. It ends with an apocalyptic vision of the end of the world as we know it, the Revelation of John.
- **E.** There were other Christian books written at about the same time as these that did not come to be included in the New Testament.
  1. One of our questions will be why these 27 books came to be privileged as sacred Scripture when the others, ultimately, did not.
  2. Another question will be how the books that did become the New Testament came to be transmitted through the ages, until the invention of the printing press could make them more widely available. (As we will see, we don't have the originals of any of the books of the New Testament, only later copies.)

V. Before getting to these questions, we should examine more closely the basic contents of the New Testament books.

- **A.** The Gospels are our earliest accounts of the life, death, and resurrection of Jesus.
  1. Scholars usually differentiate between the *synoptic* Gospels, on the one hand, and the Gospel of John, on the other.
  2. The synoptics (Matthew, Mark, and Luke) tell many of the same stories, often in the same words.
  3. John has its own set of stories and a completely different style of presentation.
  4. All four of these are to be seen as *gospels*—that is, proclamations of "good news"—rather than as objective biographies by research historians of the day.

B. The book of Acts, as well, is driven not by purely historical interests but by a powerful theological agenda: to show that God was at work in the spread of the Christian mission.

1. It traces the spread of Christianity from its inauspicious beginnings just after the death of Jesus to its auspicious arrival, after the missionary work of Paul, in the capital of the empire, Rome itself.
2. One of the questions scholars have brought to its account concerns its historical accuracy in light of its clear theological agenda.

C. The Epistles of the New Testament are usually divided into those written by Paul, on the one hand, and the *catholic* (or universal) Epistles, written by a range of authors, on the other.

1. Among the 13 letters that go under Paul's name, 7 are generally acknowledged as having come from his hand.
2. For the most part (with one exception), these deal with problems that had emerged in the churches that Paul had established as a Christian missionary in what are now Greece and Turkey.
3. Six other letters claim Paul as their author, but scholars have long harbored doubts that they were actually written by him. These so-called *Deutero-Pauline Epistles* appear to have been composed by later followers of Paul to deal with problems that had emerged in their own day.
4. There are 8 other letters in the New Testament, written by various authors to deal with a variety of problems. Here again, some of the letters (such as 2 Peter) may not actually have been written by their alleged authors. We will deal with the issue of Christian *pseudepigraphy* (the writing of books under a false name) in the course of our lectures.

D. The Revelation of John is the one apocalypse of the New Testament. We will want to explore how apocalyptic literature worked in early Christianity (and Judaism) in order to see how this book—rather than providing a blueprint for the future, as is often claimed—is best situated in its own historical context to provide a message of hope for those who were experiencing turmoil as followers of Christ.

VI. In sum, the New Testament is a much-varied and intriguing collection of books, with different authors, different genres, different audiences, different agendas, and different teachings. In this course, we will examine both the contents of these writings and the questions of how they were gathered into one canon of Scripture and handed down through antiquity until today.

Essential Reading:

Raymond Brown, *An Introduction to the New Testament*, chapter 1.

Bart D. Ehrman, *A Brief Introduction to the New Testament*, chapter 1.

Supplementary Reading:

Bart D. Ehrman, *Lost Christianities: The Battles for Scripture and the Faiths We Never Knew.*

Harry Gamble, *The New Testament Canon: Its Making and Meaning.*

Questions to Consider:

1. In your opinion, why does the New Testament continue to be such a culturally and religiously important book for people today?
2. What do you imagine would be different about our culture if all references to the New Testament were somehow removed from it?

Lecture Two

Paul—Our Earliest Christian Author

Scope: To the surprise of many readers, the *earliest* books of the New Testament were not the Gospels but the Epistles of Paul, which were produced in the 50s A.D., some 20–25 years after Jesus' death (and about 20–25 years before the Gospels). These Epistles are actual pieces of correspondence: Paul was writing letters to churches he founded in order to deal with difficulties that had arisen. Because he couldn't visit all these churches at once, his letters served as a substitute for his apostolic presence.

In this lecture, we will consider what it meant to write a letter in the ancient world. How were letters produced, published, and disseminated? What kind of writing materials (e.g., papyrus) were used? What physical form did letters take? As we will see, these questions lead to some interesting issues that affect how we understand Paul's Epistles and the other writings of the New Testament.

Outline

I. In our last lecture, we looked at the books of the New Testament in broad outline; in this lecture, we consider in a little more depth the earliest writings of the collection: the letters of the apostle Paul.

- **A.** Many people mistakenly assume that the Gospels were the first books of the New Testament to have been written.
- **B.** In fact, the letters of Paul were written at least 15 or 20 years before our earliest Gospel and are the earliest surviving writings from any Christian author.
- **C.** These are letters, for the most part, that Paul wrote to churches that he had established in Asia Minor, Macedonia, and Achaia—modern Turkey and Greece.
- **D.** In them, we learn not only about the difficulties that the Christian Church was facing in the early years of its existence but also about the life and teachings of Paul himself, who was arguably the most important figure in the history of Christianity after Jesus.

E. In this lecture, we will briefly explore the life and teachings of Paul and begin to examine the letters that he wrote, looking specifically at what it meant to write a letter in the ancient world.

II. Some have argued that without the apostle Paul, Christianity would have been radically different or, possibly, that it never would have come into existence as a major world religion.

A. Our sources for knowing about Paul's life are regrettably sparse, including the book of Acts (in which he figures prominently) and occasional references to his own past letters.

B. Paul started out not as a follower of Jesus but as an avid Pharisaic Jew who persecuted the church.

1. Early Christians maintained that Jesus was the Jewish messiah who had died for the sins of the world.
2. Most Jews did not anticipate a messiah, but some Jews thought the messiah would be a warrior who would drive out the Roman occupiers; others saw the messiah as a heavenly being; and others expected him to be a great priest.
3. No one expected that the messiah would be a crucified criminal.
4. The first Christians came to see Jesus as the messiah from their reading of passages in the Jewish scriptures that talk about one of God's righteous ones suffering for the sins of others (cf. Isaiah 53; Psalm 22).
5. These passages don't explicitly refer to the messiah, but Christians claimed they did.
6. Jews saw Jesus simply as a crucified criminal; to call him the messiah was blasphemous. This was the reason Paul persecuted the Christians.

C. But in one of the great turnarounds in all history, Paul converted from being a persecutor of the Christian Church to being its greatest advocate and missionary.

1. It appears that he had a visionary experience of Christ in the course of his own persecution of Christians.
2. This changed everything for him: He no longer saw Jesus as one who was cursed by God (in his crucifixion) but one who fulfilled God's own purposes.

3. He reasoned that Jesus' death must have had a divine purpose and concluded that Jesus' death was the way God deals with sin—it brought a right relationship with God.
4. Paul probably continued to keep Jewish Law, but came to believe that following the Law could not put a person in right standing before God; only Christ's death could do that.
5. Paul also came to believe that, Jesus' resurrection signified that the end of time was near. Paul believed, as did many Jews, that the end of time and the Last Judgment were near.
6. He believed Jesus was raised from the dead as the "first fruit," meaning that the celebration of the "harvest" (the end of time) had begun; Jesus would return to Earth in glory and this would happen in Paul's own lifetime.
7. Once convinced of this, Paul began proclaiming his new faith in Jesus as the one whose death could restore people to a right standing before God.
8. With the help of others, he began establishing churches in non-Jewish "pagan" (that is, Gentile polytheist) lands.
9. His modus operandi involved moving to an urban setting, converting pagans to believe in the one true God and Jesus as his son, forming them into worshiping communities, and then moving on to the next city to start anew.
10. When he would hear of problems in the churches he had left behind, he would write letters to them in order to deal with the problems.

III. Writing letters in the ancient world was, in many ways, similar to writing letters today, but there were some key differences.

A. Letters were often dictated, because very few people could write. (Paul, at least, knew how to pen a few words and sign his name.)

B. They could be written either on papyrus—a writing surface made out of the papyrus reed—or on wax tablets.

C. They were not mailed but hand-delivered by someone traveling to where the recipient lived.

D. They were often destroyed after they were read; if there was a reason to keep the letter, it might be copied by hand and circulated more broadly.

- **E.** Paul's letters appear to have been "read" by the churches he sent them to, which meant, necessarily, that they were read aloud in community settings.

IV. Paul's letters were, by and large, written to deal with problems of his churches, involving both how to live and what to believe.

- **A.** One clear example of a letter that is concerned with Christian lifestyle is Paul's first letter to the Corinthians.
    1. The Corinthians were experiencing numerous problems in their congregations: divisions in the church, instances of flagrant sexual immorality, questions about ethical dilemmas (such as whether it was right to eat meat that had been sacrificed to a pagan deity), and issues involving their worship services.
    2. Paul deals with each of these questions one by one, giving his pastoral advice.
    3. It is clear that the letter he writes stands in for his apostolic presence, because he could not be everywhere at once, but numerous churches depended on his insights and advice.
- **B.** An example of a letter that is concerned with proper Christian belief is Paul's letter to the Galatians.
    1. Here, the concerns are less ethical than doctrinal: Should Gentile Christians accept and follow the Jewish Law to be true members of God's chosen people?
    2. Whereas some Christian missionaries who had arrived in the Galatian community urged its members to follow the Law, Paul saw this as a real perversion of the truth of the Gospel.
    3. He urges Gentile converts not to try to attain God's favor by becoming Jewish.

V. By reading Paul's letters, we can get a sense of the kinds of problems the earliest Christian communities were experiencing, as well as a sense of the teachings and theology of Paul himself, which will be the subject of our next lecture.

Essential Reading:

Bart D. Ehrman, *A Brief Introduction to the New Testament*, chapters 12–15.

Calvin Roetzel, *The Letters of Paul: Conversations in Context*.

Supplementary Reading:

Gerald Hawthorne and Ralph Martin, *Dictionary of Paul and His Letters*.

Leander Keck, *Paul and His Letters*.

Questions to Consider:

1. Can you think of problems that might be created for interpreting Paul's teachings by the circumstance that the only way we have access to them is through personal letters he wrote?
2. Can you imagine ways Christianity would have been different if Paul had never converted to the faith?

Lecture Three
The Pauline Epistles

Scope: Now that we have some understanding about how literature was produced and disseminated in the ancient world, we can turn to the Pauline Epistles themselves to get a sense of what these, our earliest surviving Christian writings, were all about. As we will see, all of Paul's letters were *occasional* in nature—that is, they were written not in order to expound Paul's ideas in a vacuum but to address specific problems and issues that had arisen in his communities, problems related to what his fellow Christians should believe and how they should live. In this lecture, we will consider some of the major teachings of Paul's Epistles and see how he shaped his theological and ethical views in light of the problems that had emerged in his burgeoning Christian communities.

Outline

I. We have already started to examine the life and teachings of the apostle Paul, based on the materials preserved in the New Testament.

- **A.** These are our earliest and most accurate accounts: From later writings, we can learn how legends about him developed, but we have nothing from his own hand outside the New Testament.
- **B.** In this lecture, we will consider at greater length some of the key teachings of Paul and see how they came to expression in two of his important letters, the letter to the Romans and his first letter to the Thessalonians.

II. In some ways, the letter to the Romans is the best place to turn to get a sense of Paul's overarching gospel message.

- **A.** All of Paul's other letters were *occasional* (that is, motivated by certain situations that had arisen) and directed to his own churches.
- **B.** The letter to the Romans is addressed to a church that Paul did not found and had never visited.

- **C.** The occasion for the letter is indicated in its beginning and ending.
    - **1.** Paul was about to make a missionary trip to the western parts of the empire and wanted to use the Roman church as his base of operation.
    - **2.** But the Christians in Rome had heard some negative things about Paul (which shows that he was not everywhere regarded as a leading apostolic spokesperson).

III. The letter to the Romans then lays out Paul's understanding of the Christian Gospel.

- **A.** In some ways, the Gospel is predicated on "bad news" that is antecedent to the good news.
    - **1.** The bad news is that everyone, whether Jew or Gentile, is estranged from God, and there is nothing that anyone—even good, law-abiding Jews—can do to change the situation.
    - **2.** Pagans, even though they know there is only one true God, reject God; Jews, who have the Law of God, break the Law and are, therefore, no better than pagans.
    - **3.** There is no problem with the Law, only with people who are forced, by sin, to act contrary to God's will.
    - **4.** The penalty for breaking God's Law is to be alienated from God, and the Law can't solve that problem.
- **B.** The good news is that God himself has changed it by having Christ die for the sins of others.
    - **1.** Christ's death brings a reconciliation between God and his estranged people.
    - **2.** It also empowers people to do what they could not be empowered to do in any other way (for example, by keeping the Law): to overcome the power of sin to which they were enslaved.
- **C.** This teaching does not negate the teaching of the Jewish Law.
    - **1.** In fact, according to Paul, his proclamation of faith in Christ upholds the teaching of the Law.
    - **2.** This can be seen above all in the story of Abraham, the "father of the Jews," who was made right with God by faith, not by following the Law: Abraham was made right with God *before* he was given the Law about circumcision, meaning that circumcision is not necessary for a right standing with God.

3. Paul uses this example to show that salvation comes not by Law but by having faith in the promise of God, which is fulfilled by Christ's death.
4. As a result, Paul did not see himself as standing in opposition to the Jewish people, whom God would eventually save as they came to believe in the messiah God had sent.

D. Finally, even though salvation comes apart from the Law, this is not a proclamation that leads to lawlessness. Quite the contrary, those made right with God through Christ will be the ones empowered to do what God wants.

E. This, in sum, is Paul's teaching of justification by faith, apart from the works of the Law.

1. It was this teaching that stands at the heart of everything else that he said and did on his mission to convert others.
2. But most of his letters in fact deal with different issues, as these had arisen in his communities.

IV. This can be seen in his earliest letter, to the Thessalonians.

A. Paul had converted a group of pagans in the city of Thessalonica to belief in the one God and in Jesus, his son, who had died and been raised from the dead.

B. He also taught them that Christ would soon return in judgment on the earth and to bring in God's kingdom.

C. But after he left the community, some of its members had died, leading to considerable anxiety among those who were left behind: Does this mean that those who died before the kingdom had arrived had "lost out" on a chance to inherit salvation?

D. Paul's letter is written to address this question.

1. In it, he reaffirms his faith in the death and resurrection of Jesus.
2. And he gives the congregation further instruction: Those who died in Christ have not at all lost out on the promises; when Christ returns, it is they who will rise first to meet him in the air.
3. Then, all believers who are still alive will join them, entering into Christ's eternal kingdom.
4. This teaching is rooted in belief in a three-story universe: The dead are below us, and God is above us.

5. It also presupposes that the original expectation of the imminent end of the world was starting to cause some frustration among believers.

E. Paul, though, as always, worked out the implications of his gospel message for the crisis at hand, showing how in Christ God had fulfilled and would yet fulfill all his promises, by raising the dead.

V. Paul's letters were all written to speak to situations in the churches he was addressing, but at the heart of every letter, in one way or another, is his fundamental gospel message: that it was through the death and resurrection of Jesus that God had restored people to a right relationship with himself.

Essential Reading:

Bart D. Ehrman, *A Brief Introduction to the New Testament*, chapters 13 and 16.

Calvin Roetzel, *The Letters of Paul: Conversations in Context*.

Supplementary Reading:

Gerald Hawthorne and Ralph Martin, *Dictionary of Paul and His Letters*.

Leander Keck, *Paul and His Letters*.

A. J. M. Wedderburn, *The Reasons for Romans*.

Questions to Consider:

1. Try to imagine what Paul's Christian opponents might have said about his Gospel to make the Romans suspicious of him. Is there anything in his proclamation that could be caricatured to make Paul's message appear dangerous to believers?
2. Do you think Paul anticipated that the "end" would still not have come, now nearly 2,000 years later?

Lecture Four
The Problem of Pseudonymity

Scope: To this point, we have examined the authentic Pauline Epistles, that is, the letters that really were written by Paul. There are a number of other letters from antiquity that *claim* to be written by Paul but were written by someone else, for example, by a later follower of Paul who was addressing problems of his own day by taking on the authority of the apostle himself. We know of such *pseudonymous* letters from as late as the 4th or 5th century. But is it possible that some of the "Pauline" letters of the New Testament were also pseudonymous?

In this lecture, we will consider the broad problem of pseudonymity (people writing forgeries) in the ancient world, then apply our findings to the Pauline letters of the New Testament to see if any of them, in fact, were written by his followers rather than by the apostle himself.

Outline

I. In the past two lectures, we have focused on the life and letters of the apostle Paul.

- **A.** We have seen that as an early convert to become a follower of Jesus, he developed a distinctive gospel message.
- **B.** And we have seen that he molded that gospel message in his letters according to the various needs and situations that had arisen in his churches.
- **C.** Seven of his letters survive today, all of them in the New Testament.
  - **1.** We don't know when his letters starting being collected together into a group.
  - **2.** Presumably, some of the communities that he addressed kept copies of multiple letters (for example, the Corinthians), although some of these were eventually lost (cf. 1 Cor. 5:9).
  - **3.** It does appear that by the end of the 1st century, a collection of Paul's writings was already in circulation (cf. 2 Peter 3:16).

D. But letters forged in Paul's name were also in circulation from early times.
   1. Hard evidence for this can be seen in 2 Thessalonians 2:2, which speaks of a letter allegedly, but not actually, written by Paul.
   2. Some scholars think 2 Thessalonians itself was not written by Paul. If they are right, then *it* is a pseudepigraphy; if they are wrong, then the letter it refers to is. Either way, there are forged letters in Paul's name in circulation in early Christianity.
   3. There are reasons for thinking that six of the "Pauline" Epistles of the New Testament are, in fact, pseudepigraphical (that is, not actually written by Paul).

E. How can we explain the presence of forgeries among the early Christian writings? Isn't forgery a method of deception? And would highly religious, moral people engage in deception?

II. To make sense of the phenomenon of pseudepigraphy in early Christianity, we need to know something about the phenomenon more broadly in the Greco-Roman world.

A. A number of ancient writers, such as the Roman author/physician Galen, discuss the phenomenon of literary forgery.

B. The practice was relatively widespread in an age when it was difficult to decide who was the author of a literary work—especially given that a forger would naturally go out of his way to make his text sound like one written by the person whose name he was using.

C. Different authors had different reasons for forging literary texts.
   1. Sometimes, for example, there was a profit motive, when libraries would pay hard cash for "original" documents from famous authors.
   2. Sometimes, especially in some philosophical schools, an author would sign a tractate not with his own name but with the name of his teacher as an act of humility.
   3. More commonly, authors would forge a document simply in order to get a hearing for their own points of view.
   4. Even though deception was involved, therefore, there were not necessarily bad motives for forging a work.

III. We know of a number of forgeries in Paul's name from the early centuries of Christianity.

A. There is, for example, a set of letters allegedly between Paul and the most famous philosopher of his day, Seneca, who praises Paul to the hilt and indicates that even the emperor Nero was impressed with his insights.

B. And there is a *third* letter to the Corinthians that warns against certain heresies (which, as it turns out, were from the 2nd century!).

C. Is it possible that some of the writings in Paul's name that made it into the New Testament were also forged?

D. Scholars have divided the Pauline corpus into three groups.

1. There are the undisputed Pauline letters (seven altogether).
2. There are the Deutero-Pauline Epistles, which he may well not have written (2 Thessalonians, Ephesians, and Colossians). Scholars based their debate about whether Paul actually wrote these letters on consistencies of vocabulary, writing style, and/or theological beliefs.
3. And there are the pastoral Epistles, which he probably did not write (1 and 2 Timothy and Titus).

IV. The pastoral Epistles, in particular, appear to be later creations, written by a second- or third-generation follower of Paul.

A. These letters are allegedly by Paul to two of his followers, Timothy and Titus, whom he has appointed to head up churches in Ephesus and Cyprus.

1. The letters give pastoral advice about how to handle problems of internal turmoil and false teaching in their congregations.
2. They include instructions concerning what kind of men should be appointed as leaders of the churches.

B. But the letters appear not actually to be by Paul.

1. The vocabulary of these letters appears to be non-Pauline.
2. More important, the church situation that these letters presupposes does not correspond well with that in Paul's day, when there were not church hierarchies but charismatic communities run by the "spirit."

C. It appears, then, that someone in one of Paul's churches, maybe 20 or 30 years after Paul's death, wrote some letters in his name in order to deal with problems that had arisen in his own time.

D. These letters, along with those actually by Paul, came to circulate together in the apostle's name and, eventually, were included in the New Testament.

E. This conclusion—that the pastorals are pseudonymous—is important for historical reasons: The teachings of these letters may not represent what the apostle himself taught (for example, about the role of women in the churches; see 1 Timothy 2:11–15 in contrast to Galatians 3:28).

V. In sum, the New Testament appears to contain both authentic and pseudonymous Pauline letters; knowing which is which is helpful for historians wanting to know what Paul himself taught and what was taught in his name after his death.

Essential Reading:

Bart D. Ehrman, *A Brief Introduction to the New Testament*, chapters 16–17.

Calvin Roetzel, *The Letters of Paul: Conversations in Context*.

Supplementary Reading:

J. Christiaan Beker, *The Heirs of Paul: Paul's Legacy in the New Testament and in the Church Today*.

Gerald Hawthorne and Ralph Martin, *Dictionary of Paul and His Letters*.

Questions to Consider:

1. Why do people continue to forge literary works in our own day? Are the motivations different from those of antiquity?
2. Is a forged work, in your opinion, automatically not to be trusted? Why or why not?

Lecture Five

The Beginnings of the Gospel Traditions

Scope: At this point in the course, we will shift our focus away from the early Epistles of the New Testament to the books that are even more familiar to most readers: the Gospels. The Gospels differ from the Epistles in numerous respects. For one thing, each Epistle was written by one author who sat down to compose a letter, but the Gospels are filled with stories about Jesus that had been in circulation for years—decades even—before they came to be written down.

In this lecture, we will consider the beginnings of the Gospel narratives in the oral traditions that were spread throughout the Mediterranean in the years after Jesus' death. Where did these traditions come from? How did they get modified in the process of their transmission? How can we know whether the traditions that came to be written down by the writers of the Gospels are historically accurate or if, instead, they had come to be altered over the years when passed on by word of mouth?

Outline

I. To this point, we have considered some of the Epistles of the New Testament. We can now turn our attention to the New Testament Gospels.

- **A.** Even though the Gospels appear as the first books of the New Testament, they were not the first books to be written.
  - **1.** As we have seen, most of Paul's letters were written in the 50s A.D.
  - **2.** The earliest Gospel was Mark, written about a decade later, probably A.D. 65–70.
  - **3.** Matthew and Luke were probably 10–15 years after that (A.D. 80–85), and John, about 10 years after than (A.D. 90–95).
- **B.** And obviously, with the Gospels, we are dealing with a different genre of literature.
  - **1.** These are not pieces of correspondence but narratives that tell the stories of Jesus' life, ministry, death, and resurrection.

2. They are called Gospels because they are narratives with a point: They proclaim the "good news" (the literal meaning of the word *gospel*).
3. It would be a mistake, however, to think that, in terms of genre, they are unique writings from the ancient world; in fact, they appear very much like other ancient biographies of important men.
4. Ancient biographies focused less on names and dates than modern ones, and they give no sense of formative influences on a person or on the psychological development of his or her character. Instead, they tend to show key events of a person's life to give a sense of what he or she was really like.
5. One of the things that makes the New Testament Gospels unlike other religious biographies of the ancient world is that their focus is far more on the death (and resurrection) of their main character; some readers have called the Gospels "passion narratives with long introductions."

II. Even though the Gospels go under the names of Matthew, Mark, Luke, and John, they are, in fact, written anonymously.

A. The titles in our English Bibles are later additions; they are not original to the Gospels themselves.

B. Notice that the Gospel narratives are always written in the third person.

C. The identity of their real authors must remain unknown.

1. The tradition that they were written by two disciples (Matthew and John) and by two companions of the apostles (Mark and Luke) is first attested in the 2nd century.
2. What we can say for certain about the authors is that they were all highly educated, literate, Greek-speaking Christians of (at least) the second generation.
3. Contrast this with the apostles of Jesus, who were uneducated, lower class, illiterate, Aramaic-speaking peasants.
4. It seems probable, then, that none of the Gospels was actually written by one of Jesus' closest followers.
5. Where and how, then, did the writers acquire their information about Jesus?

III. Because the Gospels are not eyewitness accounts to the things Jesus said and did (they never claim to be that!), they appear to be based on oral traditions that had been in circulation about Jesus for the decades between his life and the time the Gospels were written.

A. The one thing we know about Christianity during the 30–65 years between Jesus' death and these first accounts of his life is that it rapidly spread throughout the Mediterranean.

B. As believers in Christ converted others to the faith, they told them stories about what Jesus had said and done.

C. These stories were, therefore, in circulation year after year, told in different languages and in different countries from that of Jesus.

D. What happens to stories that circulate orally for years? Obviously, they come to be changed in the retelling.

1. It should not be thought that because the ancient Roman world was an oral culture, great care was taken to preserve stories accurately.

2. Cultural anthropologists have shown that this concern for exactitude is a feature of written cultures; it would be a mistake to impose it onto oral cultures.

3. Storytellers in oral cultures recognize that stories need to be modified to fit the occasion for which they are told.

E. There is solid evidence that the stories about Jesus were modified over time, before being written in the Gospels, and that, in fact, some of the stories are not historical at all.

F. The evidence comes in the discrepancies that one finds between the same story told by different authors.

G. Some of the discrepancies have to do with minor details, such as: When did Peter deny Jesus? When the Jewish leader Jairus came to seek Jesus' help, had his daughter already died or not?

H. Some discrepancies involve more important matters: Did Jesus cleanse the Temple at the beginning or end of his ministry?

I. Some differences have an important bearing on how we understand the Gospels or how we understand Jesus' message and mission: When did Jesus die? Did Jesus ever preach about himself? Was he willing to do miracles as a sign of his identity?

IV. Eventually, the stories in circulation came to be written down.

A. Sometimes, the Gospels are remarkably alike in their written accounts—evidently, because some of them used the same written sources.

B. Yet they are all distinct from each other, as well.

C. Thus, each Gospel needs to be considered on its own terms to see what its perspective on Jesus is, rather than interpreted as providing the *same* perspective as each of the other Gospels.

Essential Reading:

Richard Burridge, *What Are the Gospels? A Comparison with Greco-Roman Biography.*

Bart D. Ehrman, *A Brief Introduction to the New Testament*, chapter 4.

Supplementary Reading:

Martin Debelius, *From Tradition to Gospel.*

W. J. Ong, *Orality and Literacy.*

Questions to Consider:

1. Have you ever heard a story told about something you did that was obviously changed from the way it really happened? Is it implausible that the same thing happened with the stories about Jesus?
2. If hundreds of new converts throughout the Roman Empire are telling stories about Jesus, would there be any way to guarantee that all the stories reflected events as they actually happened?

Lecture Six
The Earliest Gospels

Scope: It was probably about 30 or 40 years after the death of Jesus that our earliest surviving accounts of his life were produced. These are the Gospels of the New Testament: Matthew, Mark, Luke, and John. Even though we continue to call these books by the names of these authors, the accounts themselves are completely anonymous—it was only in later times that Christians reading these books attributed authors' names to them.

In this lecture, we will consider such critical matters as when these books were written, what sources of information were available to their authors, what their overarching messages are, whether there are any discrepancies among their accounts, and whether they can be trusted as reliable historical documents.

Outline

I. We have already learned a good deal about the New Testament Gospels.

- **A.** They were written about 35–60 years after Jesus' life.
- **B.** Although they are anonymous, they were written by highly educated Greek-speaking Christians.
- **C.** These authors had evidently acquired their stories principally through oral traditions in circulation about Jesus after his death.

II. It is important that each Gospel be allowed to have its own say concerning who Jesus was.

- **A.** The discrepancies among the Gospels are important not so much for their own sake (to show that there *are* discrepancies), but because they show us that each Gospel is different.
- **B.** If we try to make all the Gospels say the same thing, then we are, in a sense, writing our own Gospel, unlike any of the four that happen to survive in the New Testament.
- **C.** The differences among the Gospels sometimes affect some of the most important and familiar stories they tell.

1. For example, the accounts of Jesus' birth in Matthew and Luke are strikingly different from each other.
2. In addition to major discrepancies in Luke's and Matthew's versions of the birth of Jesus, and his family's relocation from Bethlehem to Nazareth, there are historical problems.
3. These include the nature of the miraculous star in Matthew that leads the wise men to the exact location of Jesus' birth, and the census in Luke that required knowing where one's ancestors were from. Moreover, this census involved the entire Roman Empire, and there is no account of such a huge census anywhere except in Luke.
4. And the accounts of Jesus' death in Mark and Luke are strikingly different.

D. We are best served, then, by allowing each author to tell his story of Jesus in his own way.

III. The Gospel of Mark portrays Jesus as the suffering Son of God whom no one recognizes until the very end.

A. Even though Jesus does numerous fantastic miracles in this Gospel, no one seems to recognize his identity.

B. When Peter finally confesses Jesus to be the messiah, halfway through the Gospel, even he does not realize what this means.

C. It is not until Jesus is crucified that anyone sees that *he* is the one who must suffer and die, and that is not even one of his disciples but the centurion overseeing his crucifixion!

IV. The Gospel of Matthew portrays Jesus as the Jewish messiah sent from the Jewish God to the Jewish people in fulfillment of the Jewish Law.

A. The Jewishness of this Gospel can be seen in the opening, with the genealogy of Jesus.

B. It is also seen in the numerous instances in which the author indicates that Jesus has fulfilled Scripture.

C. Strikingly, in this Gospel, Jesus insists that his followers keep the Jewish Law—even better than the highly religious scribes and Pharisees.

V. The Gospel of Luke portrays Jesus as a Jewish prophet who comes to be rejected by his own people, so that his message is then taken to the Gentiles.

A. His account of Jesus' genealogy traces his line all the way back to Adam—the father of the entire human race (not just of the Jews).

B. The first major event in Jesus' ministry is his rejection by his own people in Nazareth.

C. For Luke, this rejection was necessary because Jesus was the true prophet and, as a prophet, he knows everything that must happen to him and is not, therefore, anxious or discomfited in the face of death.

VI. The Gospel of John portrays Jesus as the one who came from heaven to teach the truth that can bring eternal life to all who believe.

A. In John, Jesus does not preach about the coming kingdom of God but about his own identity.

B. Unlike in the synoptics, he is more than willing in this Gospel to do miracles as signs that what he says about himself is true.

C. Here, Jesus is a divine man whose words bring eternal life.

VII. Each of the four Gospels is a different account of Jesus and must be studied on its own terms to see what it has to say about the meaning of his life and death.

Essential Reading:

Bart D. Ehrman, *A Brief Introduction to the New Testament*, chapters 5–7, 9.

Robert Kysar, *John the Maverick Gospel*.

Keith Nickle, *The Synoptic Gospels: Conflict and Consensus*.

Supplementary Reading:

David Aune, *The New Testament in Its Literary Environment*.

Questions to Consider:

1. People today would never assume that two different contemporary authors mean the same thing, even if their writings were included in a single anthology. Why do you suppose the authors of the Bible are treated differently?
2. Is the portrayal of Jesus in any one of the Gospels a bit surprising to you in any way? Why or why not?

Lecture Seven
The Other Gospels

Scope: Whereas most people are familiar with Matthew, Mark, Luke, and John, many do not realize that there were other Gospels written by early Christians, other accounts of Jesus' words and deeds, his death and resurrection. Why were these other Gospels not included in the New Testament?

In this lecture, we will discuss these other Gospels as a group—when they were written, who were their authors, whether they contain historically reliable information—before considering a couple of the more important and earliest "other" Gospels, written not long after the books of the New Testament themselves were produced.

Outline

I. Whereas most people are familiar with Matthew, Mark, Luke, and John, many do not realize that there were other Gospels written by early Christians.

- **A.** These are other accounts of Jesus' words and deeds, his death and resurrection. Why were these other Gospels not included in the New Testament?
- **B.** In this lecture, we will discuss these other Gospels as a group—when they were written, who their authors were, and whether they contain historically reliable information.
- **C.** We will then consider several of the more important and earliest "other" Gospels, written not long after the books of the New Testament themselves were produced.

II. The word *gospel* has both a general and a technical sense.

- **A.** In its general sense, as we have seen, the word literally means "good news."
- **B.** Early on in Christianity, though, the word came to be used of certain kinds of books that conveyed this "good news," that is, accounts of Jesus' words and/or deeds.

C. In this technical sense, there are a number of Gospels that survive from Christian antiquity.

III. In fairly recent times, people have become aware of the fact that we have a number of non-canonical Gospels.

A. In probably the most popular work of fiction in recent times, *The Da Vinci Code*, we are told that there were "eighty Gospels" that were "vying for a place" in the New Testament.

B. In point of fact, we don't know how many other Gospels were written in antiquity, whether 80 or 800.

C. What survive are about 25–30 other Gospels, many of them highly fragmentary.

D. These date from the 2nd century and extend down through the Middle Ages and on till today, where occasionally one still finds Gospels being forged and passed off as authentic.

E. For historians of early Christianity, the most interesting of these other Gospels are the earliest ones, which date from not long after the time when those of the New Testament were produced.

1. Is it true, though, that these other Gospels were vying for a spot in the New Testament and that, in many instances (as also indicated in *The Da Vinci Code*), they contain more accurate historical information than the ones that made it into the New Testament?

2. The easiest way to get a sense of the character and historical value of these non-canonical accounts of Jesus' words and deeds is by examining individual instances. Here, we will consider three of the earliest non-canonical Gospels: the Infancy Gospel of Thomas, the Gospel of Peter, and the Coptic Gospel of Thomas.

IV. The Infancy Gospel of Thomas is our first surviving account of Jesus' life as a young boy.

A. The account begins with him as a five-year-old who likes to play and who can use his supernatural powers to have fun.

B. But he has a mischievous streak and ends up using his power in order to hurt those who irritate him.

C. In the end, he manages to heal all those he has injured and raise from the dead all those he has killed, becoming subservient to his parents and using his powers for the good.

D. Even though this text is relatively ancient—coming from the early to mid-2nd century—there does not seem to be much historical information here; instead, the account has been formed by a pious, or not-so-pious, imagination about what the miracle-working Son of God must have been like as a boy.

V. The Gospel of Peter comes to us only in a fragment discovered in the 19th century in the tomb of a Christian monk.

A. The account begins with Jesus' trial before Pilate and ends with his resurrection appearances.

B. There are many similarities between this account and those in the New Testament Gospels, although it is difficult to determine whether this author made use of those earlier accounts or not.

C. Most striking are the differences between this account and the others.

1. Here, for example, it is the Jews who are *completely* at fault for the death of Jesus.
2. And there are legendary details added, such as the robber who reviled the soldiers for mistreating Jesus and who was punished, on the cross, by not having his legs broken.
3. There are some passages that could be taken in a "heretical" way to suggest that Christ did not really suffer.
4. Most striking of all, there is an actual account of Jesus' emergence from the tomb, taller than a skyscraper, with the cross emerging from the tomb behind him.

D. Here again, rather than having a historically reliable version of Jesus' life, we clearly are in the realm of later Christian imagination.

VI. Probably the most important Gospel discovered in modern times is the Coptic Gospel of Thomas, found among a cache of manuscripts in upper Egypt in 1945.

A. This book contains 114 sayings of Jesus, many of them familiar from the New Testament Gospels, but others of them very peculiar.

B. Scholars continue to debate every aspect of this book and its sayings, some claiming that it predates our canonical Gospels, but most finding its accounts of Jesus' words to be later, possibly early 2nd century, and influenced by such Christian movements as early Gnosticism.

VII. In short, there were other Gospels available to Christians of the 2nd, 3rd, and later centuries.

A. For the communities in which these Gospels were read, they no doubt constituted "Scripture."

B. But few of them enjoyed the wide distribution or favor of those that eventually came to be included in the New Testament.

C. Moreover, most of them are quite late in comparison with the canonical texts and more obviously filled with legendary accretions to the life and teachings of Jesus.

D. As a result, the four Gospels that made it into the New Testament appear, as a rule, to be the oldest and most widely used accounts of Jesus from Christian antiquity.

Essential Reading:

Ron Cameron, *The Other Gospels: Non-Canonical Gospel Texts.*

Bart D. Ehrman, *The New Testament: A Historical Introduction to the Early Christian Writings*, chapter 12.

Supplementary Reading:

John Dominic Crossan, *Four Other Gospels: Shadows on the Contours of the Canon.*

J. K. Elliott, *The Apocryphal New Testament: A Collection of Apocryphal Christian Literature in an English Translation.*

Questions to Consider:

1. In light of what we've seen in this lecture, is there any reason to think that the Gospels of the New Testament are themselves free from later imaginary accretions instead of "pure" historical "fact"?
2. What, in your judgment, is the value of knowing about the other Gospels?

Lecture Eight

Apocalypticism and the Apocalypse of John

Scope: Probably the most intriguing and least understood book of the New Testament is the Apocalypse of John, otherwise known as the Book of Revelation. In it is described the future course of history, in which widespread disaster and calamity strike the earth until the very end of time, when God intervenes in the affairs of the world to destroy the forces of evil and establish his perfect utopian kingdom on earth.

But is this book actually giving a description of events yet to transpire? This lecture seeks to place the Book of Revelation in its own historical context, to see how it would have made sense to readers of the first century, who were imbued with a religious perspective known as apocalypticism and who would have understood the symbolic descriptions of the Apocalypse to have applied to events transpiring in their own day.

Outline

I. Now that we have discussed the Epistles and Gospels of early Christianity, we can move to consider one other genre represented in the New Testament: the apocalypse.

II. There were numerous apocalypses written in the ancient world, even though today people are, by and large, familiar with only one of them, the Apocalypse of John (also known as the Book of Revelation).

- **A.** As with all genres, the apocalypse had set forms and features, which if understood, can help explain any particular book of the genre.
- **B.** One thing that all apocalypses have in common is that they set forth, in narrative form, an apocalyptic worldview.
- **C.** Thus, it is necessary to learn something about this worldview—sometimes called *apocalypticism*—if we are to make sense of a literary genre that presupposes it.

III. The worldview of apocalypticism can best be understood by tracing the history of its development in ancient Israelite thought.

A. In very early times, many Israelite thinkers subscribed to a kind of *covenantal* worldview, which claimed that God was on the side of Israel, had made a covenant with Israel, and would always protect Israel from its enemies.

B. This covenantal worldview was severely challenged by the events of history, when Israel did not appear to be protected at all.

C. There emerged a *prophetic* worldview that explained Israel's ongoing sufferings: According to the prophets, Israel suffered as a punishment for its sins; if it would return to God, he would relent, and Israel would once again thrive and prosper.

D. This prophetic worldview itself came to be severely challenged by the events of history, as some Jews realized that even after repenting, they continued to suffer and that those who were evil, on the contrary, actually prospered.

E. The apocalyptic worldview rose from the ashes of fallen prophecy. According to apocalypticists, the people of God suffer not because they are being punished for sin, but because there are powers of evil in the world who are opposed to God and his people, who are intent on destroying all those who side with God.

F. More specifically, apocalypticists subscribed to four major tenets:

1. Dualism: They maintained that there were forces of good and evil in the world, and everyone sided with one or the other; moreover, history itself was dualistic, with this present age governed by evil powers, but the age to come to be governed by all that is good.
2. Pessimism: Given that the forces of evil were in charge of this world, things were only going to get worse.
3. Vindication: But at the end of this age, God would intervene to overthrow the forces of evil and bring in his good kingdom. At that time, he would raise all those who had died, and they would face judgment. The evil would be subjected to eternal punishment, but the good would be granted an eternal reward.
4. Imminence: For Jewish apocalypticists, this coming kingdom of God was right around the corner, to arrive at any time. Therefore, people needed to prepare for it by repenting and turning to God.

IV. One way this apocalyptic worldview was conveyed was through a literary genre, the *apocalypse*.

A. Like all literary genres, the apocalypse had certain characteristic features. In general, it was an account of visionary experiences that explained the suffering of the present age in view of heavenly realities.

B. More specifically, apocalypses shared certain literary features:

1. Most (not all) of them were pseudonymous, written in the name of a religious person from the past.
2. This person is given a set of visions that usually contain some very bizarre imagery.
3. The visions are normally explained by a heavenly angel.
4. The visions are not meant to be taken literally but are symbolic statements about either what was happening now on earth or what would happen in the near future. The angelic explanations sometimes provided the key to interpreting the symbolism.
5. These apocalyptic visions typically have a triumphalist ending: God will ultimately prevail!
6. Their function, as a rule, was to encourage believers to hold and keep the faith, because their present sufferings would soon be vindicated.

V. When the Book of Revelation is read as an ancient apocalypse, its message makes considerable sense.

A. In terms of its basic plot, John, an earthly prophet, is shown the heavenly realities about what is soon to transpire on earth: disaster, catastrophe, and rampant destruction, until the very end, when Christ returns in judgment upon evil and all those under its sway.

B. The most important point to stress is that this was not written as a blueprint for our own future: It was written for Christians of the time.

C. This can be seen especially in the symbolism that comes to be explained by the angelic mediator in the book.

1. As an example: The whore of Babylon in chapter 17 refers to the political and economic exploitation the world was experiencing under the power of Rome.

2. And the Antichrist—666—is a reference to the first anti-Christian emperor, Caesar Nero, the letters of whose name actually add up to 666.

D. The point of the book was that those experiencing hardship and persecution at the time were to hold on just a little while longer, because God would soon intervene in history, overthrow the forces of evil, and bring his good, eternal kingdom to earth.

VI. The Book of Revelation was a book for its own time, and it should not be ripped out of its own historical context and made to speak about something that its author did not have in mind at all, our own future here at the beginning of the 21st century, some 1,900 years after it was composed.

Essential Reading:

Bart D. Ehrman, *The New Testament: A Historical Introduction to the Early Christian Writings*, chapter 28.

J. Pilch, *What Are They Saying about the Book of Revelation?*

Supplementary Reading:

Adela Yarbro Collins, *The Power of the Apocalypse.*

Christopher Rowland, *The Open Heaven: A Study of Apocalyptic in Judaism and Early Christianity.*

Questions to Consider:

1. Why do you suppose so many readers of the Book of Revelation are inclined to see in it a prediction of what is to happen in our own future?
2. How does situating Revelation in its own historical context affect your understanding of the book?

Lecture Nine

The Copyists Who Gave Us Scripture

Scope: In the previous lecture, we saw how the early Christian writings, including those of the New Testament, were circulated, but *why* were they circulated? What about these books made Christians eager to read and study them?

As we will see in this lecture, one of the things that made Christianity novel in the ancient world is that it was a religion largely based on books (this wasn't true of other Roman religions). Books were important because Christianity developed into a religion based on *authority*—originally the authority of Jesus, then of his apostles. But when the apostles were no longer living, what could serve as the authoritative basis of the faith? It was the books the apostles left behind. However, there were numerous books that *claimed* to be written by apostles but weren't (the pseudepigrapha). The decision about which books to accept as authoritative was a decision that had profound effects on the beliefs and practices of the early Christians.

Outline

I. Now that we have looked at some of the more important writings of the New Testament—Gospels, Epistles, and the apocalypse—we can take a step back and ask how these writings actually came down to us today.

- **A.** We need always to remember that in the ancient world, the production and dissemination of books was quite different from today.
  1. There were no printing presses, photocopy machines, or electronic transfers of information.
  2. For books to be distributed, they had to be reproduced, and they could be reproduced only by hand, one word, one letter, at a time.
  3. Not only was this a slow and painstaking process that disallowed the mass production of books in the modern sense, but it was also a process prone to errors.

4. Anyone copying a book out by longhand will make mistakes; those who wish to see can try it for themselves!
5. This means that in the ancient world, when there was more than one copy of a book, there was no guarantee that the multiple copies would be alike in all their details; odds were that they would, in fact, be different from one another.

B. We do not have the originals of any of the letters of Paul, the Gospels, or the apocalypse—indeed, of any early Christian text.

1. What we have are copies, the vast majority of them produced centuries after the originals from copies that were also centuries removed from the originals and that had themselves been made from earlier copies.
2. Dating back to AD 125-140, the earliest manuscript in existence is written on papyrus in codex form (like a book); it is called P52 because it is the 52nd papyrus that has been catalogued.
3. Starting in the 4th century, scribes copied documents on to parchment.
4. We don't have complete books of the New Testament on any surviving manuscripts until about the end of the 3rd century.
5. We don't have complete copies of the New Testament until the 4th century, 300 years after the books themselves were written.
6. Of the thousands of copies of the New Testament that now survive, most date from the Middles Ages, and no two are exactly alike in all their wording (with the exception of the smallest surviving fragments).

C. Scribes who copied the Christian texts obviously changed them. This leads to a host of interesting questions that we will address in this lecture.

1. Why were the originals of the New Testament changed in copying?
2. How extensive are the changes?
3. How many copies do we now have?
4. If all of them contain mistakes, are there places where we don't know what the authors originally wrote?

II. The fact that the originals do not survive was occasionally noted during antiquity and the Middle Ages, but it was not until relatively modern times that it was recognized as a major problem.

A. On occasion, early Christian authors commenting on the text of Scripture will point out that different manuscripts have different texts in some places.

B. And scribes in the Middle Ages would sometimes correct a manuscript they were copying from some other manuscript.

C. But it was not until after the invention of the printing press—when printers had to decide which form of the text to set up in type—that the vast differences among our manuscripts came to be recognized.

D. A major breakthrough occurred in 1707, with the publication of an edition of the Greek New Testament by Oxford scholar John Mill.

1. Mill had spent 30 years of his life comparing the Greek manuscripts of the New Testament available to him and considering the ancient translations of the New Testament into other languages and the quotations of the New Testament by the early church fathers.
2. He compiled all his results and published an edition of the New Testament that included an "apparatus" of variant readings he had discovered, that is, places where there were significant differences among the manuscripts.
3. To the shock and dismay of many of his contemporaries, Mill's apparatus indicated 30,000 places of variation. And these were only the variant readings he considered "significant" (others that he knew about, he didn't include)!

E. Since then, scholars have uncovered many more variant readings among our manuscripts.

1. Mill had examined 100 manuscripts. Today, we have well over 5000 manuscripts available.
2. As a result, we don't actually know how many variant readings survive; no one has been able to count them all.
3. Perhaps it is easiest to put the number in comparative terms. We know of more variants in our manuscripts than there are words in the New Testament.

III. There are a variety of ways to describe the differences among our manuscripts.

A. Some variants appear to have been made by accident; others, intentionally (by scribes wanting to modify the texts).

1. Accidental changes would include such relatively innocent differences as changes in spelling, the omission of a word or line, or the accidental rearrangement of words.

2. Intentional changes would include places where scribes modified the text because they thought it contained an error or a reading that was problematic.

B. Some of these variants—especially the intentional ones—are significant for understanding the meaning of the text.

1. Was the story of Jesus and the adulteress in John 8 originally found in the Fourth Gospel, or was it added later?

2. Were the last 12 verses of Mark, where Jesus appears to his disciples after his resurrection, original or added later?

3. Did Jesus pray for his executioners to be forgiven "for they don't know what they are doing," as found in some manuscripts of Luke but not in others?

4. When Jesus was approached by a leper to be healed in Mark 1, did he feel compassion for the man or did he get angry?

IV. Given the variety of our manuscripts and the mass of scribal changes in them, scholars have had to devise ways of determining what the original text was wherever there is variation.

A. Some of the criteria textual critics use involve the character of the manuscripts supporting one reading over another: Which reading do the oldest manuscripts have? Which reading is found more broadly throughout the tradition? Which reading is found in our "best" manuscripts?

B. Other criteria involve the nature of the individual readings themselves: Which readings are more in line with the writing style, vocabulary, and theology of the author otherwise? Which ones would have been more likely seen to be "better" to a scribe? (The reading that is more difficult is usually through to be the one that is original, because scribes are more likely to have tried to resolve a problematic statement than to create one.)

C. Using these criteria, we can, in most instances, be reasonably sure that we know what the authors originally wrote. But there will always be places where we are not sure.

V. It is important to remember when we read the New Testament that we are not reading the originals as produced by the ancient authors. We are reading translations into English of Greek texts whose originals do not survive; these translations are based on copies of the originals, and all of these copies have errors in them. In some places, we may not even know what an author originally said.

Essential Reading:

Bart D. Ehrman, *Misquoting Jesus: The Story Behind Who Changed the Bible and Why.*

———, *The New Testament: A Historical Introduction to the Early Christian Writings*, chapter 29.

Supplementary Reading:

Bruce M. Metzger and Bart D. Ehrman, *The Text of the New Testament: Its Transmission, Corruption, and Restoration.*

David Parker, *The Living Text of the Gospels.*

Questions to Consider:

1. In your opinion, is the "authority" of the New Testament affected by the circumstance that we don't have the originals and, in some places, may not know what the original authors actually wrote?
2. Why do you suppose the early Christians did not bother to preserve the original texts of the New Testament writings?

Lecture Ten

Authority in the Early Church

Scope: The need to have written authorities for faith and practice is ultimately what drove Christians to construct a *canon* of Scripture—that is, a collection of books that were seen to be authoritative for what to believe and how to live. From the very beginning, Christians already had one canon in that they accepted the books of the Jewish Scriptures (the Christian Old Testament) as an authoritative account of God's word. But soon there was a need for additional, distinctively Christian authorities, and this is what led Christians to consider some of the writings of the apostles (such as Paul and the authors of the Gospels) as standing on an equal footing with the writings of the Old Testament.

But given the varying understandings of the Christian religion, there were a variety of books from which to choose. How did Christian leaders know which books to include in this "New" Testament?

Outline

I. In the last lecture, we noted that the early Christian writings were in wide circulation, but we haven't explored yet the more basic question of why they were so widely circulated.

- **A.** This may seem like an obvious question, but it is one that rarely gets asked.
  - **1.** Why were the Christians so interested in the literature being produced in the early years of the religion?
  - **2.** Why did some of this literature come to take on a kind of sacred status among Christians?
  - **3.** And when did this happen?
- **B.** One reason this question does not get asked much is that people today simply assume that religions are rooted in religious texts; thus, Christianity would have been as well, from the beginning.
- **C.** But the idea that a religion would be rooted in sacred texts was virtually unheard of in the Roman world.
  - **1.** Roman religions were not textually based.

2. In Christian circles, Christianity is thought about in doctrinal terms (beliefs).
3. Roman religions were not rooted in belief, but in practice: It was the worship of the gods that mattered, not what one believed about the gods.
4. These religions were rooted around the idea that what mattered in life were the things that the gods controlled, and humans could not, such as rain, and good health.
5. Roman religions were based on present life, not on afterlife. Most people in the ancient world did not believe in an afterlife; for them, the purpose of religion was to guarantee quality of life in the present.
6. Religions in the ancient world were polytheistic, and designed to maintain peace with the gods.
7. The one partial exception, of course, was Judaism. Judaism was monotheistic, practice-based, more than belief-based, and had a sacred Scripture.
8. And the Jews' sacred Scripture soon became the Christians' sacred Scripture.
9. But why did Christians begin to regard other writings also as Scripture?
10. We will consider the entire process by which a group of Christian books became the sacred canon of the New Testament in our final lecture. In this lecture, we will consider the broader question of why Christians sought written authorities in the first place.

II. The place to begin is with one of the truly exceptional features of Christianity in the Roman world. This was an exclusivistic religion.

A. Exclusivistic religions were virtually unknown in the polytheistic world of the Roman Empire.

B. Even Judaism is only a partial exception, because not even Jews were eager to convert others to their own faith.

C. But from the beginning, Christians insisted that there was only one right religion, only one way to be right with the one true God, and only one set of beliefs that could be acceptable to him.

D. The belief in Jesus as the messiah became the *sine qua non* for Christians at the earliest stages of the religion.

E. This means that belief and its corollary, knowledge, became central to the early Christian Church.

F. Anyone with the wrong beliefs or the wrong knowledge was, therefore, estranged from God.

G. As a result, it was imperative to have the right beliefs and the right knowledge.

III. Christianity became a text-based religion because it was a belief-based religion.

A. If what mattered was proper beliefs, one needed to know what things to believe.

B. This, in turn, presupposed having authority for knowing what to believe.

C. The ultimate authority, of course, was Jesus. After his death, authority naturally descended upon his disciples. But as they were scattered and eventually died, what could take their place as authorities? The answer was: The books they left behind.

IV. Problems arose as different Christian groups believing different things all claimed to have the correct understanding of the religion (that is, claimed to represent the views of Jesus and his followers).

A. One of the most important "discoveries" of modern scholarship is that early Christianity was, in fact, remarkably diverse in its beliefs.

B. The various beliefs of Christians into the 2nd and 3rd centuries make the modern-day diversity of Christian denominations and theologies pale by comparison.

C. We can see this variety of early beliefs by exploring the ideas of two significant Christian groups of the 2nd century.

1. The Ebionites maintained that Jesus was the Jewish messiah sent from the Jewish God to the Jewish people; as a righteous man (and only a man), he had been chosen by God to die for the sake of others, but he was not himself divine or born of a virgin.

2. The Marcionites maintained that the Jewish God was not the God of Jesus but was a God of wrath who had created this miserable world, then condemned people for not keeping his Law. Jesus came from a different, good God to save people

from the Jewish God of wrath. He was not actually human (belonging to this creation) but was himself completely divine.

3. Why didn't the Ebionites and the Marcionites simply read the New Testament to see that their views were wrong? Because the New Testament did not exist yet. It came into existence as a response to these conflicts, not prior to them.

D. It is striking that each of these groups actually claimed scriptural authority for their views.

1. The Ebionites had something like Matthew, the most "Jewish" of our Gospels, and rejected Paul as an arch-heretic.
2. The Marcionites had something like our Luke, the most "non-Jewish" of our Gospels, and accepted Paul as the ultimate authority.

E. Eventually, both groups were declared heretical, and a different view emerged as victorious that agreed on some points with both groups and disagreed vehemently on others. It was this group that gave us the Scriptures that are accepted as canonical today (as we'll see in Lecture Twelve).

V. In sum, Christianity became a text-based religion because it invoked the need for proper belief, and proper belief required proper knowledge, and proper knowledge required established authorities, and authorities that are written are, in theory, more "certain" than those that are merely spoken, because their words are then cast in permanent form, available to anyone with eyes to see.

Essential Reading:

Bart D. Ehrman, *The New Testament: A Historical Introduction to the Early Christian Writings*, chapter 1.

———, *The Orthodox Corruption of Scripture: The Effect of Early Christological Controversies on the Text of the New Testament*, chapter 1.

Supplementary Reading:

Walter Bauer, *Orthodoxy and Heresy in Earliest Christianity.*

Bart D. Ehrman, *Lost Christianities: The Battles for Scripture and Faiths We Never Knew.*

Harry Gamble, *The New Testament Canon: Its Making and Meaning.*

Questions to Consider:

1. Why do you suppose today that people simply assume that all major religions are based on sacred texts?
2. If Christianity from early times was "text-based," why do you suppose Christians didn't go to greater lengths to copy the surviving texts accurately?

Lecture Eleven

The Importance of Interpretation

Scope: Even as Christians began to agree on which books were to be accepted as authoritative, in the process of forming a new canon of Scripture, they were confronted with a basic problem: It is one thing to *have* a book that is considered authoritative, but it is another thing to *interpret* the book. And as Christians have long realized, interpretations of authoritative books vary widely, sometimes radically, with different readers claiming that the book means different things.

In this lecture, we will consider the ways early Christians tried to interpret their authoritative texts, taking special note of the movement among numerous Christian readers to take their texts not just literally but also figuratively. But figurative readings—though used by nearly all early Christians—created a problem: If a text means something other than what it says, how can you control its interpretation to prevent a "false teacher" from using it to his own ends?

Outline

I. We saw in the previous lecture that Christianity from the outset was a text-based religion and that Christians, therefore, had to decide which books were to be considered sacred. But knowing which books are sacred provides no guarantee that everyone will agree on what to believe.

- **A.** The problem is that different interpreters can interpret the same book in different ways.
  1. This is obvious even today, given that different Christians from different churches interpret the New Testament in radically different ways.
  2. And this is true not just of the New Testament or other sacred books but of all books altogether. Just consider the wide-ranging interpretations of Shakespeare or the American Constitution!

3. The problem is that written texts are never self-interpreting. They always require human beings to interpret them, and humans have different views, beliefs, values, priorities, worldviews, ideas, and so on—and all these things affect how one reads a text; thus, the same text can mean different things to different people.

B. For early Christians to ensure that the "right" beliefs would be held, they had to do more than choose which books were authoritative; they also had to determine how these books were to be interpreted.

II. The problem was well recognized in the early centuries of Christianity, as different groups interpreted the sacred Scriptures in radically different ways.

A. The famous "heretic" Marcion, for example, used a literal interpretation to discredit the writings of the Hebrew Scriptures, which for other Christians were the sacred "Old Testament."

1. Marcion based his views on the writings of Paul, who differentiated between the Law and the Gospel.
2. For Marcion, this was an absolute distinction, to the point that the God who gave the Law to the Jews was obviously not the same God who provided salvation from the Law through Jesus.
3. Marcion wrote a book called the *Antitheses* (meaning "contrary statements"), in which he showed that the teachings of the Jewish Bible contradicted the teachings of Jesus.
4. His conclusion was that it was the Gospel of Jesus, as proclaimed by Paul, that was to be observed; the Jewish Bible was not to be accepted as Christian Scripture.

B. Other allegedly false teachers, such as the Gnostics, did not opt for a literal interpretation of texts but moved into highly figurative modes of interpretation.

1. Gnostics maintained that this world was an evil place in which portions of the divine (our inner selves) had come to be trapped in matter (our bodies). The point of their religion was to provide escape by transmitting the "knowledge" (*gnosis*) that is necessary to escape our imprisonment.
2. For Gnostics, there are three kinds of people in the world: pure animals that have no afterlife; people (such as normal

Christians) who can have faith and do good works, and will have an afterlife as a reward; and elite Christians (Gnostics) who had a heavenly pre-existence. When they are set free by the "saving knowledge" they will return to the realm whence they came.

3. Behind the idea of salvation by knowledge lay a set of complicated myths that explained how this world and the world of the divine beings came into existence.
4. One of these myths talks about an unknowable God; we cannot know him because our knowledge is restricted to our senses and this God is immaterial.
5. Divine beings called Aeons emanated from this God; the twelfth divine being was Sophia (wisdom) who tried to understand the divine realm and overreached her grasp; she fell from the divine world and in her fall, conceived an imperfect offspring, the creator of the material world.
6. This demiurge declared he was the only God (the God of the Old Testament). He and his minions split up his mother, Sophia, into a million pieces, which became entrapped in human bodies. Thus, some humans have a "divine spark" of Sophia in them.
7. Sophia longs to be set free and in order for this to happen the people with the "divine spark" of Sophia in them need to know how they came to be on Earth and how they can return to the divine world they came from.
8. Gnostics believed they had the power to receive this sacred knowledge which could come only from a being from the divine world, i.e.: Christ
9. The Gospel of John portrays Jesus as a divine being who comes to earth to reveal the divine truth necessary for salvation, a view that was very amenable to Gnostics.
10. Orthodox Christians opposed the Gnostic interpretation of John, just as they opposed Gnostic interpretations more broadly, because Gnostics were inclined *not* to accept the literal understanding of the Scriptures. They believed that just as Sophia is trapped within the body, so too, truth is entrapped beneath the literal words of a text.
11. Some of the Gnostics' interpretations of Scripture were used to support their myths. For example, some Gnostics believed

that there were 30 divine beings in the divine realm, who had all emanated from the one true God. Evidence came in the circumstance that Jesus started his ministry when he was 30 years old.

12. The idea that the 12th divine being was the one whose fall from the divine realm is what led to the creation of this miserable material world was shown by the fact that it was Jesus' 12th disciple, Judas Iscariot, who betrayed him.
13. Church fathers responding to this kind of teaching stressed that the Gnostic figurative interpretations of Scripture had nothing to do with their literal meanings.
14. In an effective image used by the church father Irenaeus, the Gnostic interpretations of Scripture are like someone taking a gorgeous mosaic of a king, rearranging its stones into the image of a dog, and claiming that's what the artist had in mind all along.

C. Even proto-orthodox church leaders used figurative modes of interpretation when it suited them, however.

1. The church father Barnabas, for example, interpreted the laws of Jews, including circumcision, Sabbath observance, and kosher food laws, as symbolic statements of what people should believe and how people should behave, rather than as literal laws to be followed.
2. Thus, even though proto-orthodox Christians emphasized the need to interpret texts literally in order to know what God meant to teach them, they, too, used figurative modes of interpretation when it suited their purposes.

D. Despite this ambivalence on the proper approach to interpretation, it can be said that for most proto-orthodox leaders, the literal mode of interpretation was to be given preference to the symbolic in trying to decide what the Scriptures really mean.

III. The debates over interpretation continued for centuries.

A. Throughout most of Christian history, figurative interpretations were sanctioned and encouraged.

B. Eventually, with the Reformation and the Enlightenment, the literal approach to interpretation came to be championed and privileged, until today, when it seems simply like the "commonsensical" way to read texts.

C. But we should always remember that "common" sense simply means the sense shared by the majority of persons at any given time. Commonsense views are not necessarily true; they are simply widely shared.

IV. In sum, there were wide debates in the early church over how to interpret the texts of Scripture. Although these debates may have subsided, their significance has not: Christians continue to disagree in fundamental ways about what their sacred texts teach about what to believe and how to live.

Essential Reading:

Bart D. Ehrman, *The Orthodox Corruption of Scripture*, chapter 1.

Karlfried Froehlich, *Biblical Interpretation in the Early Church.*

Supplementary Reading:

Water Bauer, *Orthodoxy and Heresy in Earliest Christianity.*

Robert M. Grant and David Tracy, *A Short History of the Interpretation of the Bible.*

Questions to Consider:

1. Are there any situations today in which a "non-literal" reading of a text is to be preferred over a literal one?
2. In your judgment, if church fathers disallowed a figurative interpretation of Scripture for the Gnostics, how could they deny the merit of Marcion's claim that when read literally, the texts of the Jewish Scriptures seem to present a God who is different from the God of Jesus?

Lecture Twelve
When Did the Canon Get Finalized?

Scope: In our concluding lecture, we will ask how, why, and when the canon of the New Testament came to be finalized so that we ended up with 27 books, and just these 27 books, no more and no fewer. Is it true, as stated in some popular fiction, that the 4th-century emperor Constantine made the decision about which books were to be included? Who did make the decision, and on what grounds?

In the course of this concluding lecture, we will consider some of the books that nearly made it into the New Testament but were finally excluded, such as the Apocalypse of Peter, as well as some books that did make it in but nearly did not, such as the Apocalypse of John.

Outline

I. Despite the fact that different Christians could interpret books in different ways, it became important to the proto-orthodox Christians to know which books were Scripture.

A. In part, this was because they wanted to differentiate themselves from Jews, who also had a collection of sacred books.

B. But in larger part, it was because there were competing understandings of the faith, each claiming "apostolic" authority for its views.

C. Proto-orthodox Christians then wanted to know which books should be included in a sacred canon of Scripture and which could be safely excluded.

D. The debates over which books to include and exclude were long and drawn out; the matter was not decided, in fact, for centuries.

II. There were some books that were not, ultimately, included in the New Testament that were, at one time or another, by one proto-orthodox group or another, considered Scripture.

A. This is true, for example, of the Gospel of Peter, a fragment of which was discovered at the end of the 19th century.

1. We've known about the Gospel of Peter for centuries because it was written about by Eusebius in the 4th century, but we didn't have the actual book until it was discovered in the 1860s.
2. The story that Eusebius tells is interesting because it describes a period of church history that we know little about.
3. Eusebius is sometimes called "the father of church history," because he is the first church father to write a history of the church from the days of Jesus to Eusebius' own time at the beginning of the 4th century.
4. Eusebius quotes at length a number of documents that no longer survive; among them is the story of the Gospel of Peter.
5. Eusebius tells a story about Serapian, a late 2nd century church father, who was a bishop of Antioch in Syria.
6. Serapian sanctioned the use of the Gospel of Peter by a church in Rhossus. But people told him that the Gospel of Peter contained docetic Christology.
7. When Serapian read the book, he realized that some passages could be interpreted docetically and forbad its use. Thus, the Gospel of Peter came to be excluded from the canon and disappeared.
8. The book as we have it, in any event, is very interesting, because it is the only early Gospel to give an actual account of what happened at Jesus' resurrection.

B. Another book allegedly by Peter, the so-called Apocalypse of Peter, was considered even more broadly to be part of Scripture up until the 4th century.

1. This book, too, was unavailable to us until the end of the 19th century.
2. This book is also very interesting, because it is the first surviving Christian account of someone being given a guided tour of heaven and hell, as Christ shows Peter the realms of the blessed and the damned.
3. Eventually, it too, however, was ruled out of court as containing too literalistic an understanding of the afterlife.

III. There were other books that came to be included in the New Testament that were, for many years, under a cloud of suspicion.

A. The Letter to the Hebrews, for example, was considered non-canonical by a large number of proto-orthodox Christians who did not think it was "apostolic." Not until it was accepted as authored by the apostle Paul (it never claims to be) was it received into the canon.

B. Even more problematic was the Book of Revelation.

   1. Part of the problem was uncertainty over the identity of its author.
   2. It claims to be written by John, but which "John" is not known. Its writing style is quite different from the style of the Gospel of John.
   3. Scholars continue to believe to this day that the author of the Gospel of John and the author of the Revelation of John are not the same person.
   4. Eventually some Christians argued that Revelation should not be included in the canon because its literal portrayal of a 1,000-year reign of Christ after a bloody tribulation on Earth was too naively literalistic an understanding of what would happen at the end of time.

IV. Despite the uncertainties, there was a clear movement to establish a canon of Scripture from the earliest days of Christianity.

A. At the outset, of course, the Jewish Bible was accepted as authoritative (even by Jesus himself).

B. Before the end of the New Testament period, the sayings of Jesus were considered among Christians to be at least as authoritative as the teachings of the Jewish Scriptures (for example, 1 Timothy 5:18).

C. Moreover, the writings of Jesus' apostles were sometimes granted scriptural standing, even before the New Testament period was over (cf. 2 Peter 3:16).

V. Debates over which books to include, however, lasted for centuries.

A. We know of these debates because several lists of books considered to be scriptural have survived from early Christianity, as for example, Eusebius' list of books.

   1. In the 18th century, another list of books was discovered by an Italian scholar named Muratori. The so-called "Muratorian Canon" is a list of books probably made at the end of the 2nd

century in Rome by an anonymous Christian author, who apparently considered them to be scriptural.

2. The author of the Muratorian Canon accepts 22 of the books that came to be included in the New Testament, but does not accept the book of Hebrews, James, 1 and 2 Peter, or 3 John.
3. He accepts the Apocalypse of Peter and the Wisdom of Solomon, as part of the canon, and rejects other books, including The Shepherd of Hermas because he believed it was not written in apostolic times.

B. Throughout this period, different Christians argued for the canonicity of a variety of books, based largely on four criteria.

1. A book had to be ancient (written near the time of Jesus).
2. It had to be by an apostle (or a companion of the apostles).
3. It had to be widely used throughout the church.
4. Most especially, it had to be "orthodox" (communicating the "right teaching").

C. To the surprise of many people today, the first Christian of record to maintain that the New Testament was to consist of the 27 books accepted today was the Alexandrian bishop Athanasius in A.D. 367—some 300 years after most of these books had been written!

D. Even after Athanasius's day, there continued to be disputes, until the matter was more or less resolved for most Christians around the 5th century.

E. There was no ecumenical church council that made this decision (although some local councils ratified the list on occasion). Instead, it was a matter of popular opinion, which affected, of course, which books were actually copied over time.

1. Churches and individuals were most interested in having copies of the Scripture; thus, these were the books that were reproduced more often (some of them more frequently than others; Mark, for example, was not copied nearly as often as John).
2. Other books disappeared from the scene not because there were massive book burnings, but simply because no one saw the need to copy them, and the surviving copies were lost, worn out, destroyed, or simply thrown away.

VI. With the invention of the printing press, there was no longer any question about which books would be included in the New Testament, because the same 27 books in the same sequence were copied time after time.

VII. Thus, we have our New Testament today, the collection of books that has proved more significant for the history and culture of Western civilization than any other, without rival in the West for its social and religious importance.

Essential Reading:

Bart D. Ehrman, *Lost Christianities: The Battles for Scripture and the Faiths We Never Knew.*

———, *The New Testament: A Historical Introduction to the Early Christian Writings*, chapter 1.

Supplementary Reading:

Harry Gamble, *The New Testament Canon: Its Making and Meaning.*

Bruce M. Metzger, *The Canon of the New Testament: Its Origin, Development, and Significance.*

Questions to Consider:

1. How might Christianity have been different if the Gospel of Peter or the Apocalypse of Peter had made it into the New Testament? Of if the Book of Revelation had not?
2. In your opinion, should the canon of the New Testament remain theoretically open? That is to say, should the Christian Church have the right to decide to exclude some books or to add others to the canon?

Timeline

63 B.C. .... Conquest of Palestine by the Romans.

44 B.C. .... Assassination of Julius Caesar.

40 B.C.–4 B.C. .... Herod, king of the Jews.

27 B.C.–A.D. 14 .... Octavian Caesar Augustus as emperor.

4 B.C.? .... Jesus' birth.

A.D. 14–37 .... Emperor Tiberius.

A.D. 26–36 .... Pilate as governor of Judea.

A.D. 30? .... Jesus' death.

A.D. 33? .... Conversion of Paul.

A.D. 37–41 .... Emperor Caligula.

A.D. 41–54 .... Emperor Claudius.

A.D. 54–68 .... Emperor Nero.

A.D. 50–60? .... Pauline Epistles.

A.D. 65? .... Gospel of Mark.

A.D. 66–70 .... Jewish Revolt and destruction of the Temple.

A.D. 69–79 .... Emperor Vaspasian.

A.D. 79–81 .... Emperor Titus.

A.D. 80–85? .... Gospels of Matthew and Luke, book of Acts.

A.D. 80–100? .... Deutero-Pauline Epistles, 1 Peter, Hebrews, James.

A.D. 81–96 .... Emperor Domitian.

A.D. 85–105? .... Pastoral Epistles.

A.D. 90–95? .... Gospel of John.

A.D. 95?..Book of Revelation.

A.D. 98–117 ....Emperor Trajan.

A.D. 120?......................................2 Peter.

A.D. 110–130?...............................Gospels of Peter and Thomas.

A.D. 125?......................................Infancy Gospel of Thomas.

A.D. 135 ....Letter of Barnabas.

A.D. 160–225 ....Tertullian.

A.D. 296–373 ....Athanasius.

Glossary

apocalypse: A literary genre in which an author, usually pseudonymous, describes symbolic and often bizarre visions that reveal the heavenly mysteries that make sense of earthly realities.

apocalypticism: A worldview held throughout the ancient world by many Jews and Christians that claimed that the present age is controlled by forces of evil, which would be destroyed at the end of time, when God would intervene in history to bring in his kingdom. This event was thought to be imminent.

apostle: From a Greek word meaning "one who is sent." In early Christianity, the term designated special emissaries of the faith who were representatives of Christ.

autograph: The original manuscript of a document, from a Greek word that means "the writing itself."

canon: From a Greek word that literally means "ruler" or "straight edge." The term is used to designate a recognized collection of texts; the New Testament canon is, thus, the collection of books that Christians have traditionally accepted as authoritative.

Christ: See **messiah**.

covenant: An agreement or treaty between two social or political parties. Ancient Jews used the term to refer to the pact God made with the Jewish ancestors to protect and preserve Israel as his chosen people in exchange for their devotion and adherence to his Law.

Deutero-Pauline Epistles: Ephesians, Colossians, and 2 Thessalonians, letters that have a "secondary" (Deutero) standing among the Pauline Epistles because scholars debate whether they were actually written by Paul.

Docetism: The view that Jesus was not a human being but only "appeared" to be; from a Greek word that means "to seem" or "to appear."

Ebionites: A group of second-century adoptionists who maintained Jewish practices and Jewish forms of worship.

gentile: A Jewish term for a non-Jew.

Gnosticism: A group of ancient religions, closely related to Christianity, that maintained that sparks of a divine being had become entrapped in the present, evil world and could escape only by acquiring the appropriate secret *gnosis* (Greek for "knowledge") of who they were and how they could escape. This *gnosis* was generally thought to have been brought by an emissary descended from the divine realm.

gospel: Literally, "good news." When used for a book, it refers to an account of the sayings and/or deeds of Jesus.

Greco-Roman world: The lands and culture of the Mediterranean from Alexander the Great through the early Roman Empire (c. 300 B.C. to A.D. 300).

heresy: Any worldview or set of beliefs deemed by those in power to be deviant; from a Greek word that means "choice" (because "heretics" have "chosen" to deviate from the "truth"; see **orthodoxy**).

Manuscript: Any handwritten copy of a text.

marcionites: Followers of Marcion, the second-century Christian scholar and evangelist, later labeled a heretic for his docetic Christology and his belief in two Gods, the harsh legalistic God of the Jews and the merciful loving God of Jesus—views that he claimed to have found in the writings of Paul.

messiah: From a Hebrew word that means "anointed one," which translates into Greek as *Christos* (whence our English word *Christ*). The 1st century saw a variety of expectations of what this future anointed one might look like, some Jews expecting a future warrior king like David; others, a cosmic judge from heaven; others, an authoritative, priestly interpreter of the Law; and others, a powerful prophet from God like Moses.

Muratorian Canon: An 8th-century manuscript, copied probably from a 2nd-century original, that lists the books that its author considered to belong to the New Testament canon. This is probably our earliest surviving canon list.

orthodoxy: Literally, "right opinion"; a term used to designate a worldview or set of beliefs acknowledged to be true by the majority of those in power. For its opposite, see **heresy**.

Passion: From the Greek word for "suffering." The passion is used as a technical term for the traditions of Jesus' last days, including his crucifixion (hence, the *Passion narrative*).

Pastoral Epistles: New Testament letters that Paul allegedly wrote to two pastors, Timothy (1 and 2 Timothy) and Titus, concerning their pastoral duties. Most critical scholars doubt whether Paul actually wrote them.

Proto-orthodox Christianity: A form of Christianity endorsed by some Christians of the 2nd and 3rd centuries (including the apostolic fathers) that promoted doctrines that were later declared "orthodox" by the victorious Christian party in the 4th and later centuries, in opposition to such groups as the Ebionites, the Marcionites, and the Gnostics.

pseudonymity: The practice of writing under a "false name," as is evident in a number of pagan, Jewish, and Christian writings from antiquity.

Roman Empire: All of the lands (including Palestine) that had been conquered by Rome and were ruled, ultimately, by the Roman emperor, starting with Caesar Augustus in 27 B.C. Before Augustus, Rome was a republic, ruled by the Senate.

synoptic Gospels: The Gospels of Matthew, Mark, and Luke, which tell many of the same stories, sometimes in the same words, so that they can be placed side-by-side to be "seen together" (the literal meaning of *synoptic*).

textual criticism: Any discipline that attempts to establish the original wording of a text on the basis of its surviving manuscripts.

Torah: A Hebrew word meaning "guidance," "direction," or more woodenly, "law." It is often used as a technical term either for the Law of God given to Moses or for the first five books of the Hebrew Scriptures, which were sometimes ascribed to Moses: Genesis, Exodus, Leviticus, Numbers, and Deuteronomy.

Undisputed Pauline Epistles: Romans, 1 and 2 Corinthians, Galatians, Philippians, 1 Thessalonians, and Philemon. Scholars are, for the most part, unified in judging that these letters were actually written by Paul. See also **Deutero-Pauline Epistles** and **Pastoral Epistles**.

Biographical Notes

Alexander the Great: Alexander of Macedonia, otherwise known as Alexander the Great, was one of the most influential persons in the history of Western civilization. Born in 356 B.C. to King Philip of Macedonia, he succeeded to the throne at the age of 22 upon the assassination of his father. Alexander was driven by his desire for conquest, and through real military genius and ruthless military policy, he quickly managed to conquer Greece, before moving his armies eastward to overcome Asia Minor, Palestine, and Egypt. His major conquest came over Darius, ruler of the Persian Empire, which extended his territories well into what is modern-day India.

Alexander's real historical significance is found in his use of military conquest to spread a previously unheard-of cultural unity to the lands around the Mediterranean. As a youth, Alexander had studied under the great Greek philosopher Aristotle and became convinced of the superiority of Greek culture. As a military conqueror, he actively encouraged the use of the Greek language and the adoption of Greek culture in the lands he ruled, building cities in the Greek style with gymnasia, theaters, and public baths as his administrative centers. He was particularly influential in spreading Greek ways to the upper-class elites throughout his domain. This process of spreading "Greek" (*hellas*) culture throughout the Mediterranean is called *Hellenization*. It played an enormous role in the history of Western civilization and, of course, for the New Testament, which was rooted in Hellenistic culture and was itself written in Greek.

Athanasius: Athanasius was a highly influential and controversial bishop of Alexandria throughout the middle half of the 4th century. Born around 300 A.D., he was active in the large and powerful Alexandrian church already as a young man, appointed as a deacon to the then-bishop Alexander. He served as secretary to the important Council of Nicea in 325 C.E., which attempted to resolve critical issues concerning the nature of Christ as fully divine, of the same substance as God the father, and co-eternal with the father.

As bishop of Alexandria from 328–375, Athanasius was a staunch defender of this Nicene understanding of Christ and a key player in the development of the orthodox doctrine of the Trinity, in which there were three distinct persons (Father, Son, and Spirit) who were, nonetheless, one God, all of the same substance. This defense created enormous difficulties for Athanasius in the face of powerful opposition, to which he himself reacted with a show of force (even violence). He was sent into exile on several occasions during his bishopric, spending nearly 16 years away from Alexandria while trying to serve as its bishop.

Author of numerous surviving works, Athanasius is of most significance for this course for his role in determining which books should be accepted in his churches as sacred Scripture. In 367 A.D., in his 39th annual "Festal Letter," which like all the others, set the date for the celebration of Easter and included pastoral instruction, he indicated that the 27 books that we now have in the New Testament, and only those 27, should be regarded as canonical. This decree helped define the shape of the canon for all time and helped lead to the declaration of other books, such as the Gnostic Gospels and the like, as heretical.

Barnabas: We are not well informed about the historical Barnabas. He is mentioned both by the apostle Paul (Gal. 2:13; 1 Cor. 9:6) and the book of Acts (Acts 9:27; 11:22–26) as one of Paul's traveling companions, and it appears that he was originally a Hellenistic Jew who converted to faith in Christ and became, like Paul, a traveling missionary who spread the faith. The book of Acts goes so far as to consider him one of the "apostles" (Acts 14:4, 14).

The Epistle of Barnabas discussed in this course is attributed to him, but modern scholars are reasonably sure that he could not have written it. The book appears to have been written some time around 130 or 135 A.D., some 60 years or so after the historical Barnabas would have died. The book was attributed to him, then, by Christians who wanted to advance its authoritative claims as being rooted in the views of one of the most important figures from the early years of Christianity.

Irenaeus: Irenaeus was an important theologian and heresiologist of the late 2nd century. Born probably around 130 A.D., he may have been raised in the city of Smyrna and educated, eventually, at Rome. He ended up in the Christian church of Lyon, Gaul (modern-day France), where he was made bishop around 178 A.D. He died around the year 200 A.D.

Irenaeus is our best patristic source for the Gnostic sects of the 2nd century. His best-known book is a five-volume attack on heresy, which he entitled *Refutation and Overthrow of What Is Falsely Called Gnosis*, frequently called simply *Against Heresies*. In it, he gives considerable detail concerning various heretical groups (not simply Gnostics) and, based on his understanding of Scripture and using a full panoply of rhetorical ploys and stratagems, refutes them one by one. This book was used as a source for many of the later heresiologists, including Tertullian and Epiphanius.

Jesus: We do not know when Jesus was born, but if it was during the reign of King Herod of Israel, as recorded in the Gospels of Matthew and Luke, then it must have been sometime before 4 B.C., the date of Herod's death. Jesus was raised in a Jewish home in the small village of Nazareth in Galilee, the northern part of what is now Israel. As an adult, he engaged in an itinerant preaching ministry in largely rural areas of Galilee; there is no record of him visiting any large cities until his fateful journey to Jerusalem at the end of his life. His message was comparable to that found in the prophets of the Hebrew Bible: The people of Israel must repent or they will be faced with judgment. Jesus, though, gave this message an apocalyptic twist, as did many other religious Jews of his day: The coming judgment would be of cosmic proportions and brought by an emissary from heaven, the Son of Man, who would overthrow the forces of evil and establish God's kingdom on earth. When this happened, there would be a serious reversal of fortunes; those in power now would be destroyed and those who suffered and were oppressed now would be exalted. People needed to prepare for this historical cataclysm by turning back to God and keeping his Law, especially as interpreted by Jesus himself.

Despite Jesus' reputation as a healer and exorcist, he was not viewed favorably by Jewish leaders. At the end of his life, he came to Jerusalem during a Passover feast, caused a disturbance in the Temple, and raised the ire and fears of the ruling party, the Sadducees, who were intent on keeping the peace and avoiding any riots during such tumultuous times. They had Jesus arrested and turned him over to the Roman governor, Pontius Pilate, who ordered him crucified as a troublemaker. Scholars dispute the precise year of his death, but it must have been some time around A.D. 30.

Marcion: Marcion was one of the most infamous "heretics" of the 2nd century. Tradition indicates that he was born and raised in Sinope, on the southern shore of the Black Sea, where as a young man, he acquired considerable wealth as a shipping merchant. His father was allegedly the bishop of the Christian church there, who excommunicated his son for his false teachings. In 139 A.D., Marcion went to Rome, where he spent five years developing his theological views, before presenting them to a specially called council of the church leaders. Rather than accepting Marcion's understanding of the Gospel, however, the church expelled him for false teaching. Marcion then journeyed into Asia Minor, where he proved remarkably successful in converting others to his understanding of the Christian message. "Marcionite" churches were in existence for centuries after his death, around 160 A.D.

Marcion's understanding of the Gospel was rooted in his interpretation of the writings of the apostle Paul, whose differentiation between the "Law" (of the Old Testament) and the "Gospel" (of Christ) Marcion took to an extreme, claiming that the old and new were fundamentally different, so much so that they represented the religions of different Gods. Marcion, in other words, was a *ditheist*, who thought that the Old Testament God—who had created the world, called Israel to be his people, and gave them his Law—was a different god from the God of Jesus, who came into the world in the "appearance" of human flesh (because he was not actually part of the material world of the creator-god) to save people from the just but wrathful God of the Jews. Marcion's views were based on his canon of Scripture—the first canon known to be formally advanced by a Christian—which did not, obviously, contain anything from the Old Testament but comprised a form of the Gospel of Luke and 10 of Paul's letters (all those in the present New Testament except 1 and 2 Timothy and Titus).

Paul the Apostle: Paul was a Hellenistic Jew born and raised outside of Palestine. We do not know when he was born, but it was probably sometime during the first decade A.D. Through his own letters and the encomiastic account found in the book of Acts, we can learn something of his history. He was raised as a strict Pharisaic Jew and prided himself in his scrupulous religiosity. At some point in his early adulthood, he learned of the Christians and their proclamation of the crucified man Jesus as the messiah; incensed by this claim, Paul began a rigorous campaign of persecution against the Christians—only to be converted himself to faith in Jesus through some kind of visionary experience.

Paul then became an ardent proponent of the faith and its best-known missionary. He saw his call as a missionary to the Gentiles and worked in major urban areas in the regions of Asia Minor, Macedonia, and Achaia to establish churches through the conversion of former pagans. A distinctive aspect of his message was that all people, Jew and Gentile, are made right with God through Jesus' death and resurrection and by no other means; the practical payoff was that Gentiles did not need to become Jewish in order to be among the people of the Jewish God—in particular, the men did not need to become circumcised.

We know about Paul principally through the letters that he wrote to his churches when problems had arisen that he wanted to address. There are seven letters in the New Testament that undisputedly come from his hand; six others claim him as an author, but there are reasons to doubt these claims. According to the book of Acts, Paul was eventually arrested for socially disruptive behavior and sent to Rome to face trial. An early tradition outside of the New Testament indicates that Paul was martyred there, in Rome, during the reign of the emperor Nero in A.D. 64.

Tertullian: Tertullian, from Carthage (North Africa), was one of the most influential authors of early Christianity. Much of his life is shrouded in obscurity, but it appears that he was born into a relatively affluent family of pagans, around 160 A.D., and received an extensive training in (pagan) literature and rhetoric. He converted to Christianity some time in his mid-30s and then became an outspoken, even vitriolic, proponent of the Christian faith, writing numerous works defending the faith against its cultured despisers (apologies), scathing criticisms of heretics and their beliefs, and severe tractates concerning Christian morality. At some point in his life, he joined a group of schismatics known to history as the Montanists (named after their founder, Montanus), an ethically rigorous, ascetic group that anticipated the imminent end of the world as we know it.

For this course, Tertullian is most important for his anti-heretical writings. A bitter opponent of both Gnostics and Marcionites, he is one of our best sources of information concerning what these groups, especially the latter, believed. His five-volume attack on Marcion, for example, still survives and is our principal means of access to Marcion's life and teaching.

Bibliography

Aune, David. *The New Testament in Its Literary Environment*. Philadelphia: Westminster, 1987. A superb introduction to the genres of the New Testament writings in relation to other literature in the Greco-Roman world.

Bauer, Walter, *Orthodoxy and Heresy in Earliest Christianity*. Trans. Robert Kraft et al. Philadelphia: Fortress, 1971. One of the most important books of the 20th century on the history of early Christianity. Bauer argues against the classical understanding of orthodoxy and heresy by maintaining that what was later called heresy was, in many regions of early Christendom, the oldest and largest form of Christian belief.

Beker, J. Christiaan. *The Heirs of Paul: Paul's Legacy in the New Testament and in the Church Today*. Philadelphia: Fortress, 1991. An engaging study of the Deutero-Pauline and pastoral Epistles, written by one of the leading Pauline scholars of the end of the 20th century.

Brown, Raymond. *An Introduction to the New Testament*. Anchor Bible Research Library. New York: Doubleday, 1997. This is a full and authoritative introduction to all of the major issues pertaining to the study of the New Testament, by one of the premier New Testament scholars of the second half of the 20th century. It includes extensive and up-to-date bibliographies.

Cameron, Ron. *The Other Gospels: Non-Canonical Gospel Texts*. Philadelphia: Westminster, 1982. An important collection of the earliest Gospels that did not make it into the New Testament canon.

Collins, Adela Yarbro. *Crisis and Catharsis: The Power of the Apocalypse*. Philadelphia: Westminster Press, 1984. This is a superb discussion of the authorship, social context, and overarching message of the Revelation of John.

Cross, John Dominic. *Four Other Gospels: Shadows on the Contours of the Canon*. Minneapolis: Winston Press, 1987. An intriguing discussion of four of the major early Christian Gospels that did not make it into the canon of Scripture, including the Gospels of Peter and Thomas.

Ehrman, Bart D. *A Brief Introduction to the New Testament*. New York: Oxford University Press, 2004. An introduction to all the major issues involved in studying the New Testament writings from a historical perspective, written for those coming to the study for the first time.

———. *Lost Christianities: The Battles for Scripture and the Faiths We Never Knew*. New York: Oxford University Press, 2004. A study of the wide-ranging diversity of Christianity in the 2nd and 3rd centuries, of the sacred texts (many of them forged) produced and revered by different Christian groups of the period, and of the struggles that led to the emergence of "orthodox" Christianity prior to the conversion of Constantine. For popular audiences.

———. *Misquoting Jesus: The Story Behind Who Changed the Bible and Why*. San Francisco: HarperSanFrancisco, 2005. A popular treatment of *textual criticism*, the discipline that attempts to reconstruct the "original" writings of the New Testament from the surviving manuscripts.

———. *The New Testament: A Historical Introduction to the Early Christian Writings*. 3rd ed. New York: Oxford University Press, 2004. This volume provides a historically oriented introduction to all of the issues dealt with in this course, by the instructor. It is designed both for use as a college-level textbook and as a resource for anyone interested in the New Testament.

———. *The Orthodox Corruption of Scripture: The Effect of Early Christological Controversies on the Text of the New Testament*. New York: Oxford University Press, 1993. This is a study of the ways scribes were influenced by doctrinal disputes in the early church and of how they modified their texts of the New Testament in order to make them conform more closely with their own theological views. It is best suited for more advanced students.

Elliott, J. K. *The Apocryphal New Testament: A Collection of Apocryphal Christian Literature in an English Translation*. Oxford: Clarendon Press, 1993. An excellent one-volume collection of non-canonical Gospels, Acts, Epistles, and Apocalypses, in a readable English translation with nice, brief introductions.

Froehlich, Karlfried. *Biblical Interpretation in the Early Church*. Philadelphia: Fortress, 1984. A useful discussion of the methods of interpretation prevalent in early Christianity, especially in view of their roots in other interpretive practices of the ancient world.

Gamble, Harry. *The New Testament Canon: Its Making and Meaning*. Philadelphia: Fortress, 1985. This is a clearly written and informative overview of the formation of the canon that shows how, why, and when Christians chose the present 27 books to include in their sacred Scriptures of the New Testament.

Grant, Robert M., and David Tracy. *A Short History of the Interpretation of the Bible*. Philadelphia: Fortress, 1983. A survey of the methods used to interpret the Bible from the earliest of times onward.

Hawthorne, Gerald, and Ralph Martin. *Dictionary of Paul and His Letters*. Downers Grove, IL: Intervarsity, 1993. A "Bible dictionary" with in-depth articles on a wide range of topics pertaining to Paul and his letters, written by prominent evangelical Christians.

Keck, Leander. *Paul and His Letters*. Philadelphia: Fortress, 1979. This is an insightful overview of Paul's theology, as expressed in his letters. It makes for an excellent resource for those who are new to the field.

Kysar, Robert. *John, the Maverick Gospel*. Atlanta: John Knox, 1996. This is one of the best introductions to the distinctive features of John's Gospel, which pays particular attention to how John differs from the synoptics in many of its major perspectives on Jesus.

Metzger, Bruce M., and Bart D. Ehrman. *The Text of the New Testament: Its Transmission, Corruption, and Restoration*. 4th ed. New York: Oxford, 2005. This is the classic introduction to the history, data, and methods of New Testament textual criticism, in a newly revised edition. Portions of the book require a basic knowledge of Greek, but all English readers can use the book as a tremendous resource.

Nickle, Keith. *The Synoptic Gospels: Conflict and Consensus*. Atlanta: John Knox, 1980. One of the best introductory discussions of the background and message of the three synoptic Gospels.

Parker, David. *The Living Text of the Gospels*. Cambridge: Cambridge University Press, 1997. This is perhaps the best introduction to New Testament textual criticism for beginners, in which the author argues that the modifications made by the Christian scribes who copied the text show that they did not see it as a dead object but as a living tradition.

Pilch, J. *What Are They Saying about the Book of Revelation?* New York: Paulist Press, 1978. This is a clear and useful overview of the perspectives on the Book of Revelation found among modern scholars.

Roetzel, Calvin. *The Letters of Paul: Conversations in Context*. 3rd ed. Atlanta: John Knox, 1991. This is perhaps the best available introductory discussion of the Pauline Epistles, which includes an examination of the issues of authorship and date, as well as a sketch of the major themes of each letter.

Rowland, Christopher. *The Open Heaven: A Study of Apocalyptic in Judaism and Early Christianity*. New York: Crossroad, 1982. A major overview of early Jewish and Christian apocalypticism, as evidenced in the surviving texts.

Wedderburn, A. J. M. *The Reasons for Romans*. Edinburgh: T & T Clark, 1988. The most complete book-length discussion of the reasons that Paul wrote his letter to the Romans: to explain his gospel of salvation apart from the Law to the predominantly Gentile Roman Christians, in light both of the tensions between Jews and Gentiles there and of his own impending journey to Jerusalem.

Notes

Notes

Notes

Notes

Notes